Breeders' Best™

A KENNEL CLUB BOOK®

Miniature Schnauzer

By Muriel P. Lee

BREEDERS' BEST™
A KENNEL CLUB BOOK®

MINIATURE SCHNAUZER

ISBN: 1-59378-915-7

Copyright © 2004

Kennel Club Books, LLC
308 Main Street, Allenhurst, New Jersey, 07711 USA
Printed in South Korea.

10 9 8 7 6 5 4 3 2 1

PHOTOS BY:
Paulette Braun,
Bernd Brinkmann and
Isabelle Français

DRAWINGS BY:
Yolyanko el Habanero

Contents

Meet the Miniature Schnauzer

The Miniature Schnauzer is a small ("below-the-knee"), active dog who is very popular throughout the world. In the United States, he belongs to the American Kennel Club's Terrier Group; in the United Kingdom and on the Continent, he is placed in the Utility Group of dogs.

Whether he is considered a terrier or a utility dog, the Miniature Schnauzer was bred to go to ground and to rout out the rabbits, mice and

Opposite ends of the schnauzer spectrum: the smallest of the three schnauzer breeds, the Miniature, poses with the largest, the Giant.

4

rats from the barns and sheds on the farms. To this day, those instincts are still within him whether he be in the city or in the country. Take him for a walk and he will show an immediate interest in a squirrel. Let him run a pasture in the country and he will quickly be chasing a rabbit.

A handsomely groomed solid black Miniature Schnauzer with natural ears, as is typical of European-bred dogs.

This is an intelligent and elegant dog. He will be a grand pet in addition to being a very willing worker or competitor in pursuits like obedience or agility. He fits in very well with family life whether or not you have children, and he will be equally at home in an apartment, in the suburbs or in the country. He is spirited and bright, he likes to please his family, and he has a happy outlook on life. The Mini Schnauzer is less aggressive than his terrier counterparts and much easier to train than his rather stubborn terrier cousins.

"Trixi" is a pretty salt-and-pepper hailing from Germany, the breed's homeland.

Miniature Schnauzer

The Miniature Schnauzer's roots are in Germany, and he has two older "cousins," the Giant Schnauzer and the Standard Schnauzer. The Standard Schnauzer, the original of the three sizes, can trace its history back to the 15th and 16th centuries in Germany, where he was a very able worker on the farm. He was used as a cattle dog and a guard dog and, on occasion, he was used as a ratter. As time went on, the smaller Standards were eventually crossed with the Affenpinscher, thus bringing down the size to that of the Miniature.

By the very early 1900s, Miniature Schnauzers were being registered as pure-bred dogs. In the early 1920s, Miniature Schnauzers were imported from Germany to the very famous Marienhof Kennel, the kennel that formed the breed in America. Marienhof Kennel was active for 50 years, producing over 100 champions and top winners. However, regardless of the breed's numerous wins in the show ring over the decades, the Mini Schnauzer still retains his "go-to-ground" abilities; his instincts for chasing a squirrel or a rabbit have not diminished over the generations of breeding.

By the mid 1940s, Dorothy Williams of Dorem Kennels became very active in the breed. Dorem Kennels produced 40 champions, including Ch. Dorem Display. Display made an exceptional impact upon the breed and, by the late 1990s, nearly all of the 5,000 American champions had Dorem in their background. He was a top winner in the breed and sired over 40 champions. It is unusual in any breed to have had one dog become so influential on breed type.

SIZE COMPARISON OF THE THREE SCHNAUZER BREEDS

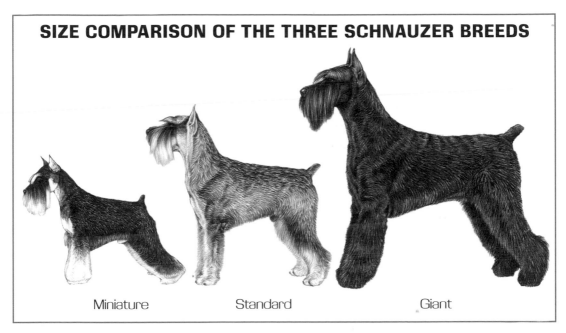

Miniature   Standard   Giant

Several other breeders should be mentioned; in fact, you might even find these names in the background of your dog's pedigree. Landis and Penny Hirsten, Penlan Kennels, have produced over 150 champions, with their dog Ch. Penlan Peter Gunn siring over 70 champions. His sire, Ch. Penlan Checkmate, was the sire of 34 champions. Mr. Hirsten is now a highly regarded terrier judge. Joan Huber of Blythewood Kennels has bred more than 200 champions in almost five decades of breeding. Ch. Blythewood Shooting Sparks was a multiple Best-in-Show winner and sired 53 champions. Mrs. Huber has been a well-known figure in the show ring for many years and continues to produce competititive dogs.

The Miniature Schnauzer is a dog that was bred to do a job. He is intelligent and likes to please his master. He

CHAPTER 1

can be a "couch potato," but his history shows that he knows how to think and that he is tough. Because he was originally bred to work, he has a mind that can understand problems and work out solutions. The Mini Schnauzer is happy doing a day's work, unlike some breeds that were bred to be companions only. And don't let his size fool you,

A Mini Schnauzer and handler relaxing "backstage" at a recent Westminster Kennel Club show. The breed is at the top of the charts in AKC registrations, beloved companions of many and popular as show dogs.

as he can hold his own when necessary and will not back down.

Having a dog that is intelligent, is a quick learner, has a steady disposition and likes to work means that you will have a pet that will be very trainable and who will want to please you. In obedience and agility classes across the country, you will see many Miniature Schnauzers working with their masters. In addition to earning the basic degrees, Mini Schnauzers will be found winning titles at the most difficult and demanding levels of agility and obedience competition.

The Miniature Schnauzer may have outstanding working ability, but he has also done very well in the show ring. Although his coat for the show ring requires a substantial amount of grooming, once the finished product reaches the ring, a good Miniature Schnauzer will almost always be in the

Meet the Miniature Schnauzer

winners' circle.

Whether looking for an obediencc dog, a dog for the show ring or a dog to join your family circle, the Miniature Schnauzer is hard to beat! In the US, the Miniature Schnauzer consistently places in the top 15 in popularity of the over 150 AKC breeds. AKC registrations well exceed 20,000 annually. In the UK and in Europe, he is equally popular. This is certainly a breed to consider when adding a pet to the household.

Lapdog size plus much bigger ability and personality make the Mini Schnauzer a favored choice.

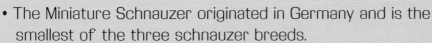

MEET THE MINIATURE SCHNAUZER

Overview

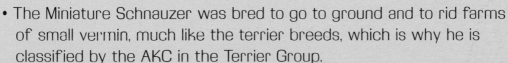

- The Miniature Schnauzer originated in Germany and is the smallest of the three schnauzer breeds.
- The Miniature Schnauzer was bred to go to ground and to rid farms of small vermin, much like the terrier breeds, which is why he is classified by the AKC in the Terrier Group.
- The Miniature Schnauzer is a tough, intelligent and athletic dog, popular around the world for his convenient size, sparkling personality and myriad abilities.
- The breed's registration numbers are among the highest with the AKC and English Kennel Club, as well as in Continental Europe.

CHAPTER 2

Description of the Mini Schnauzer

E very breed of dog has an official standard, which gives a detailed written description of what the breed should look, act and move like. Although the standard of the American Kennel Club can be slightly different from the standards of other national registries in different countries around the world, there will be great similarities, as all Mini Schnauzer standards aim to describe essentially the same dog.

The American standard describes

The Miniature Schnauzer may be small and compact, but he is a robust and sturdily built dog.

the Miniature Schnauzer as a "robust, active dog of terrier type, resembling his larger cousin, the Standard Schnauzer, in general appearance, and of an alert and active disposition." Dogs are no taller at the shoulder than 14 inches and bitches are no more than 12 inches. There is a disqualification for dogs under 12 inches and over 14 inches. There is no weight given in the standard, but an adult bitch of 13 inches will weigh about 14 pounds, and males are slightly heavier than females.

A typical crop-eared Mini Schnauzer. The distinct facial furnishings, complete with beard and eyebrows, give the breed an unforgettable expression.

In color, the breed can be salt and pepper of all shades (combination of black and white banded hairs), black and silver or solid black. Salt and pepper is still the most popular of the three colors, and it has been only in the more recent years that there have been black and silver and all-black champions. In the US, the only white permitted is a small white spot on the chest of the black dog. White patches

The popular salt-and-pepper coloration can vary in its shadings from dog to dog.

on the body of any of the colors is unacceptable. Solid white is not a recognized color in the US and UK, although it is an approved color in Europe.

In the United States, ears can be cropped or uncropped. When uncropped, the ear will fold close to the head. Nearly all show dogs in the US will have cropped ears, as it is very difficult to finish a Mini Schnauzer to his championship with uncropped ears.

The close of the American standard notes, "The typical Miniature Schnauzer is alert and spirited, yet obedient to command. He is friendly, intelligent and willing to please. He should never be over-aggressive or timid." On the other side of the Atlantic, the English standard describes the dog as, "Sturdily built, robust, sinewy, nearly square (length of body equal to height at shoulder). Expression keen, attitude alert." He is "well balanced, smart, stylish and adaptable." Of course, the Mini Schnauzer is known worldwide for being reliable and intelligent.

The standard used by Europe's Fédération Cynologique Internationale (FCI) is that of Germany, the breed's homeland. Major differences between the AKC and FCI standards include the aforementioned inclusion of the solid white coloration in the FCI standard, and also the requirement for natural ears only in the FCI standard. Ears in the FCI standard are described as "drop ears," and there is no mention of ear cropping. Cropped ears are not permitted in the UK either. Another difference is that the FCI classifies the Mini Schnauzer in its Group 2, in a subsection for "Pinscher and Schnauzer type," rather than as a terrier. The Mini Schnauzer is a Utility breed in the UK, which is comparable to the AKC's Non-Sporting Group, comprising breeds that serve mainly as companions today and whose intended functions vary widely.

What you should now be aware of is that the Miniature Schnauzer, no matter from what part of the world he comes, is basically, because of his size, a good "town dog," with his height around 12 inches to 14 inches at the shoulder and his weight around 12 to 15 pounds. He is a popular breed among those who live in urban areas and apartments. He is active and smart. He is compact in shape and size, but he still needs to be kept active and challenged. He also will require grooming. The Mini Schnauzer's popularity is largely due to his being "personality-plus" and adaptable to most any living situations due to his size.

A natural-eared youngster from Germany in solid white. While this color is not accepted by the AKC, it is recognized throughout Europe according to the German standard, which is the standard used by the FCI.

DESCRIPTION OF THE MINI SCHNAUZER

Overview

- A breed standard is an approved official document that describes the ideal physical characteristics, movement and temperament of that breed.
- The Miniature Schnauzer is seen in three colors in the US and UK, with solid white as a fourth approved color in Continental Europe.
- The Miniature Schnauzer is a small, compact breed, packing a lot of personality and ability into a convenient size for most any living environment.
- The Miniature Schnauzer is popular around the world and is classified differently by different national registries: as a terrier in the US, as a utility breed in the UK and with other schnauzer types and pinschers on the Continent.

Are You a Mini Schnauzer Person?

Before purchasing your Miniature Schnauzer, you should really think about the personality and characteristics of this breed to determine if this is the right dog for you. Answer the following questions and, if you can answer each one positively, you are off to a good start. You might also like to attend a local dog show. Find out what time the Mini Schnauzer is being shown and, after the judging,

The Mini is ever-alert to the goings-on around him, whether he's patrolling on watchdog duty or just looking out the window to see his beloved owner returning home.

talk to some breeders and handlers and take the opportunity to see the Miniature Schnauzers "up close."

The questions you should consider are:

1. Do you have time to give to a dog? He will need care, companionship, training and grooming. This is almost like having a child, except that a dog remains childlike in that he will always require your care for his well-being.

2. Are you looking for a small dog, one that weighs 15 pounds or less?

3. Do you have a fenced-in yard for your dog? If not, will you be willing and able to walk your dog several times a day?

4. Are you willing to give your new pet a weekly brushing and a full grooming every two or three months? Are you aware that this is a breed that requires a fair amount of grooming and that, if you are unable to do it yourself, you will

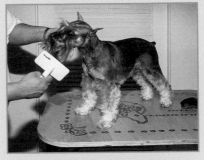

Don't forget the grooming! Wiry coats like the Mini's require special attention to stay in healthy condition and proper texture, and the heavy facial furnishings must be kept neat and clean.

Owners of the Miniature Schnauzer love their dogs' "big-dog" personalities and talents packed in a compact size that makes them easy to bring along.

have to take your pet to a professional groomer?

5. Are you willing, or able, to have a dog that tends to be a bit noisy? Will your neighbors tolerate this? The Miniature Schnauzer, a good watchdog, does tend to be a bit noisier than other breeds.

Let's look at each question in more detail, one at a time.

1. Time for a dog does not mean that you cannot work and own a dog. Your new pet will need quality time, just like a child needs it. A dog must be fed and exercised several times a day, on a regular schedule. He needs to be cuddled and loved. He will like to go places with you whenever possible. He will really like it if you work with him in a sport that requires some intelligence and athletic ability.

The dog should have at least two good outings a day, and that means a walk in the morning and evening if this is an apartment dog. A dog with a fenced-in yard needs adequate time to romp and play. Never let your dog out loose, even if you live on a very quiet street with little traffic, as it only takes one car or truck to run down your four-footed family member.

2. If you are looking for a lap-sized dog and another family member wants a dog that weighs 75 pounds, talk it over. Make certain that all members of your family will be happy with the smaller dog. The advantages of a smaller dog are many. He can sit in your lap. He does not drool. Clean-up in the yard is much easier as the feces, like the dog, are small! If you so desire, a small dog can easily sleep in your bed. There's also a lot less to

The Mini is a playful and busy dog but can adapt to any type of living environment provided his owners give him sufficient opportunity for exercise and time outdoors in safe areas.

Miniature Schnauzer

groom! Visitors to your home can be overwhelmed by a large dog who jumps up to greet them, while they often think that a bouncy small dog is cute and fun. And a small dog can be as good a watchdog as a larger breed. Small dogs

However, Miniature Schnauzers do very well in apartment life. As adults, they will only need to be taken out for bathroom breaks three or four times a day. A reminder: when walking your dog, it is essential to carry a plastic bag to pick

Mini Schnauzer fanciers often find it hard to own just one! These pals lounge around on their very own doggie cot, which is slightly raised to protect them from drafts.

will eat much less than large dogs, costing less to maintain.

3. If you have a fenced-in yard, you will find it very easy to toilet-train a dog. The dog can easily be let outside for his potty time whenever needed.

up droppings. These can easily be tossed in a handy trash receptacle on your way home.

4. The Miniature Schnauzer is a "coated" breed. His coat will grow long and straggly without proper care. If not kept up, the

coat will become matted, and he will no longer look the way he should. You must have the time and patience to brush your dog once a week. Every two or three months, the pet Miniature Schnauzer should be taken to the groomer to be trimmed so he looks like a true representative of his breed.

5. As a responsible dog owner, it is up to you to make certain that your dog is trained not to bark needlessly. The Miniature Schnauzer can be a bit noisy, but it is not fair to your neighbors to leave your dog outside to bark endlessly. With the Mini Schnauzer's trainability, this, if a problem, can be easily stopped.

If you answered *yes* to these questions, you are on your way to becoming a Miniature Schnauzer person!

ARE YOU A MINI SCHNAUZER PERSON?

Overview

- You must thoroughly consider your decision before beginning your puppy search. Are you ready for dog ownership, and is the Miniature Schnauzer the right breed for you?
- Think about pros and cons: the Mini Schnauzer is a bright, personable, conveniently sized companion, but he also needs coat care—and he can be a barker.
- Do you have the time and finances to properly care for and maintain a dog? This dog will become part of your family, requiring attention every day and necessitating changes to your daily routine.
- Once you've decided, the fun part can begin—picking your new family member!

CHAPTER 4

Selecting a Breeder

Healthy, sound, sturdy, clean pups, brimming with Schnauzer personality, are what you expect to see when visiting a reputable breeder.

When you buy your Mini Schnauzer, you will want a healthy puppy from a responsible breeder. A responsible breeder is someone who has given a lot of thought before breeding his bitch. He considers health problems in the breed, he has room in his home or kennel for a litter of puppies, and he has the time to give to a litter. He does not breed to the dog down the block because it is easy and because he wants to show his children the miracle of puppy birth. A good breeder is not just a breeder but also a fancier, someone who is involved in the dog sport, an active member of the AMSC and his regional breed club. Breeders either show their own dogs or have professionals or associates handle their dogs. A reputable breeder only breeds a bitch who has earned a championship in the ring, indicating that she is of superior quality to produce progeny to help improve the breed.

Good breeders provide their pups with opportunities for early socialization. A pup's adjustment to life in a human pack will be easier if he has already been exposed to well-behaved youngsters of various ages.

The American Miniature Schnauzer Club (AMSC) describes responsible breeders as follows: "Knowledgeable about their breed, screen for genetic diseases, should offer a written guarantee and offer information and assistance. They usually belong to a local or national breed club where they can network with other knowledgeable breeders. They breed for temperament, good health and soundness."

A responsible breeder is someone who is dedicated to the breed and to breeding out any faults or hereditary

A good time to meet experienced breed folk is during down time at a show. A breeder's involvement in showing, breed clubs and other breed activities attests to her dedication to the Miniature Schnauzer.

problems, and whose overall interest is in improving the breed. He will study pedigrees and go to dog shows to see what the leading stud dogs are producing. To find the right stud dog for his bitch, he may fly the bitch across the country to breed to a particular stud dog, or the breeder may drive the bitch to the dog, who may be located a considerable distance away. The breeder may only have one or two litters a year, which means that there may not be a puppy ready for you when you first call. Remember that you are purchasing a new family member, so take your time! Usually the wait will be well worthwhile.

The responsible breeder will be involved in the Mini Schnauzer scene on a local and national level. Look for a breeder who belongs to the American Miniature Schnauzer Club as well as the local Miniature Schnauzer club if there is one in the area. This is the breeder that you are likely to meet at your local all-breed dog show. Responsible breeders show their dogs. They compare their breeding to that of other breeders, and they also like to see good-quality dogs of other breeders. These ethical breeders are always striving to breed out any genetic problems in the breed. They are always working to improve their dogs, in both conformation and health issues.

Once you've chosen a breeder, you will go for a visit. The breeder will show you his kennel, if he has a kennel, or will invite you into his home to see the puppies. The areas will be clean and smell good. The breeder will show you the dam of the puppy that you are looking at, and she will be clean, good-smelling and groomed. The puppies will also be clean and groomed up to look like little Miniature Schnauzers. The breeder may only show you

The breeder will also have questions for you: Have you had a dog before? How many have you had and have you ever owned a

Now here's dedication! This breeder has turned the yard into agility training grounds and is right there working the dog. If looking for a future competition dog, seek out a breeder who is successful in your areas of interest.

one or two puppies, as he will not show you the puppies that are already sold or that he is going to keep.

schnauzer? Did your dogs live long lives? Do you have a fenced yard? How many children do you have and what are their ages?

Do not be offended by these questions. The breeder has put a lot of effort and money into this litter. His first priority is to place every pup in a caring household where the pup will be wanted, loved and cared for.

The breeder will supply you with your pup's health and vaccinations records and will show you the records of testing that he has had done on the parents to prove that they are genetically clear of certain problems. The breeder will also have a blue AKC registration slip for your puppy. You will take this home with you when you pick the puppy up, as proof that the puppy has been registered with the AKC.

With a popular breed, such as the Miniature Schnauzer, you can contact local breed clubs, as there are many around the country and they can assist you in finding a puppy. The AMSC website will give you the names, addresses and

Minis hanging out next to their Giant housemate, in his crate. If your breeder does raise more than one breed, it should be a related breed like these schnauzer cousins.

phone numbers of these individuals, and you can always contact the national club's breeder referral service to point you toward contacts in your area. National clubs of all breeds are very anxious to assist newcomers to the breed by educating them, helping them to find the right puppies and making good matches between families and puppies. The American Miniature Schnauzer Club's website is http://amsc.us. This site offers a wealth of information on the breed and what the club does to further the breed's best interests. Furthermore, the American Kennel Club's site (www.akc.org) will give you quantities of information on all breeds of dog, including the Miniature Schnauzer.

SELECTING A BREEDER

Overview

- Your first step in picking your puppy is finding a responsible, ethical breeder, truly dedicated to the best interests of the Miniature Schnauzer and actively involved in the breed.
- The American Miniature Schnauzer Club is the breed's AKC parent club and an excellent resource to help you get started with bringing a Mini Schnauzer into your life.
- Good breeders focus on health, soundness and temperament as well as physical conformation in planning their matings, only breeding from top-quality dogs in all aspects.
- Have stringent requirements when selecting a breeder. Likewise, a good breeder will have rigorous requirements for new owners and will interview prospects to ensure that each and every puppy goes to a good home.

Finding the Right Puppy

The new puppy is like a new child in many respects! He is dependent on his human pack for all aspects of his care, which of course includes lots of cuddles from his new mom, dad and siblings.

You are now ready to select your puppy. You have decided that you are a Miniature Schnauzer person and you like a smaller, active, intelligent dog. You are willing to groom your dog regularly and to take him to a professional groomer if and when it's necessary. Your entire family is ready for this new arrival into your home and your lives. You have done your homework and have located a responsible breeder who has a litter available.

You arrive at the appointed time

and the breeder has the puppies ready for you to look at. They should be a happy bunch, clean and groomed. Their noses will be wet, their coats will have a glow or sheen and they will have a nice covering of flesh over their ribs. They will look and act like cute-as-a-button Miniature Schnauzer puppies!

The breeder may have had five or six pups in the litter, but he is only showing you the pups that are available for sale. He may only show you the pups that he thinks would be best for your family. Reputable breeders raise each litter and each puppy equally. Each puppy will have the same genetic background, and each pup will have received equal quality time from his mother and from the breeder. A pup may be mismarked or not have quite the right tail set, but he will still be just as good a companion in a pet home. Do not expect to find a Best-in-Show dog

It's doubtful that you'll get mom and pups to pose for a happy family portrait like this when you visit the litter, but all pups should be healthy, friendly and eager to meet you. Their dam should likewise be healthy and of good temperament despite the stresses of raising a litter.

The whole family should play a role in selecting the new addition, so bring along the kids once you've found a suitable breeder and litter.

on your first time out to purchase a pup! However, you should be able to find a super puppy that will become a happy, healthy member of your family as long as he lives. You don't a show-quality pup to have a great companion, just one that is healthy and sound.

Some breeders will have the temperaments of their puppies tested by either a professional, their veterinarian or another dog breeder. They will find the high-energy pup and the pup that is slower in responding. They will find the pup with the independent spirit and the one that follows the pack. If the litter has been tested, the breeder will suggest which pup he thinks will be best for your family. If the litter has not been tested, you can do a few simple tests while you are sitting on the floor with the pups.

Pat your leg or snap your finger and see which pup comes up to you first. Clap your hands and see if one of the litter shies away from you. See how they play with one another. Watch for the one whose personality appeals most to you, as this will probably be the puppy that you will take home. Look for the puppy that appears to be "in the middle," neither overly rambunctious nor submissive. You want the joyful pup, not the wild one. Spend some time selecting your puppy. If you are hesitant, tell the breeder that you would like to go home and think it over. This is a major decision, as you are adding a family member who may be with you for 10 to 15 years. Be sure you get the puppy that you will all be happy with.

There is another option, and that is to adopt a "rescue" Miniature

Schnauzer. This will be a Mini Schnauzer who, for whatever reason, is looking for a new home. This will usually be a dog over one year of age and very often trained and housebroken. The breed rescue organization will bathe and groom the dog in addition to having a veterinarian's health certificate attesting to the good health of the dog. Usually these dogs make marvelous pets, as they are grateful for a second chance at a loving home. Not only does the national club have an active rescue organization, but the local affiliates will also have groups of individuals working in this capacity. Rescue committees consist of very dedicated individuals who care deeply about the breed and give countless hours of their time and money to rescue, provide foster homes and seek out good new permanent homes for these dogs.

FINDING THE RIGHT PUPPY

Overview

- Once you've found a breeder, it's time to visit the litter and meet the puppies.
- The litter and parents should all be in good health and should receive much attention from the breeder. The areas in which the dogs are kept should be clean.
- Part of the fun is getting to know each pup's personality and finding the one that is your perfect match.
- For those who'd rather skip the puppy stage, adopting an adult Mini Schnauzer from a rescue organization is a great way to add the breed to your life while giving a dog another chance at a good home.

Welcoming the Mini Schnauzer

You have now selected your puppy and are ready to bring your new family member home. Before welcoming your pup, you should buy food and water pans and a leash and collar. You should also consider purchasing a crate for your puppy not only to sleep in but also to spend time in when he is home alone or otherwise unsupervised for a few hours. In very short order, your puppy will learn that the crate is his second home. He will feel safe and secure when he is in the crate. When the pup is left

Ear-cropping is usually done when the pups are just a few days old, and this youngster's ears already are standing nicely. Your breeder will give you any necessary instructions for after-care of the ears.

uncrated and alone, he will quickly become bored and begin to chew on things like the furniture and the corners of the woodwork. Keeping him in a confined area when you are not around can eliminate these problems. You will also need several towels or a washable blanket to add to the crate so that he will be comfortable.

Your Mini Schnauzer does not need very large food and water bowls, but he does need sturdy, chew-proof bowls that are easy for you to clean.

If you are driving some distance to pick up your pet, take along a towel or two, a water pan and your leash and collar. Also take along some plastic baggies and a roll of paper towels in case there are any potty accidents or motion sickness.

HOME SAFETY AND THE FIRST FEW DAYS
Before bringing your puppy into the house, you should be aware that a small puppy can be like a toddler and there are dangers in the household that must be eliminated. Electrical wires should be raised off the floor and hidden from view, as they are

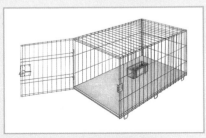

A wire crate, which is the most popular type of crate for use in the home, is one of the most important tools in your pup's training and safety. Purchase a crate for your pup that will comfortably house him as an adult.

very tempting as chewable objects. Swimming pools can be very dangerous, so make certain that your puppy can't get into, or fall into, the pool if you have one. Barricades will be necessary to prevent accidents. Not all dogs can swim, and those with short legs like the Mini cannot climb out of the pool. Watch your deck railings and make sure that your puppy cannot slip through the openings and fall.

If you have young children in the house, you must see that they under-stand that the small puppy is a living being and must be treated gently. They cannot handle him roughly, pull his ears or pick him up and drop him. This is your responsibility. A child taught about animals at an early age can become a lifelong compassionate animal lover and owner.

Use your common sense in all of these issues.

Consider where a young child can get into trouble, and your puppy will be right behind him!

When your pup comes into the house for the first time (after he has relieved himself outside), let him look at his new home and surroundings. Give him a light meal and some water. When he is tired, take him outside for another potty trip and then tuck him into his crate, either to take a nap or, hopefully, to sleep through the night.

The first day or two for your puppy should be fairly quiet. He will then have time to get used to his new home, surroundings and family members. The first night he may cry a bit, but if you put a soft puppy-safe toy or a soft woolly sweater in his crate, this will give him some warmth and security. A nearby ticking clock or a radio playing soft music can also be helpful. Remember,

The most important thing you can have in your home for your new Mini is lots of love!

he has been uprooted from a sibling or two, his mother, and his familiar breeder, and he will need a day or two to get used to his new family. If he should cry this first night, let him be and he will eventually quiet down and sleep. By the third night, he should be well settled in.

If you have other pets in your home, be careful in introducing the new puppy to them. The cat may hide for a few days, but he will eventually come out. If you have an elderly dog in poor health, you must not allow the puppy to tease him. Have patience and, within a week, it will seem to you, your family and your puppy, that you have all been together for years.

PUPPY SUPPERTIME
Choosing a suitable food is another consideration for the new owner. Nutrition for your puppy is actually very easy. Dog-food companies

hire many scientists and spend millions of dollars on research to determine what will be a healthy diet for your dog at each stage of life. Your breeder should have been feeding a premium puppy food, and you should continue on with the same brand. As the dog matures, you will change over to the adult formula of the same brand. Do not add vitamins or anything else unless your veterinarian suggests that you do so. Do not think that by cooking up a special diet you will turn out a product that will be more nutritious than what the dog-food companies are providing.

Your young puppy will probably be fed three times a day and perhaps as many as four times a day. As he starts growing, you will cut his meals to two times a day, in the morning and in the evening. By the time he reaches about eight months

There are many types of cute carriers available for puppies and small dogs, but you should give your Mini Schnauzer time to settle in before introducing him to the great big world. You also should check with your vet to see that your pup is properly vaccinated before going out and about.

of age, you will be changing over to the adult-formula food. You can check your dog-food bag for the amount, per pound of weight, that you should be feeding your dog. To the dry kibble, you can add a splash of water to moisten and possibly a tablespoon or so of a canned dog food for flavor. Keep the table treats to a minimum; you don't want to encourage begging or obesity, and some "people foods" are harmful to dogs. Give him a dog treat at bedtime and small bits of treats as rewards. Keep a good covering of flesh over his ribs, but do not let your dog become a fat boy!

A few treats will help your puppy settle in and associate good things with you, his new leader.

However, the more active the dog, the more calories he will need. Always have fresh drinking water available. This may include a bowl of water in the kitchen and another outside in the yard.

You are now off to an excellent start with your puppy. As the days go by, you will quickly find more items that you will need, including several tough chew toys and a retractable leash for walks in the park once he walks politely on a regular lead. You will need grooming supplies and a good pooper scooper. These items can be acquired as needed from your local pet-supply shop.

Puppy-proofing your home means indoors and out. Don't grant your pup access to areas where chemicals, fertilizers and dangerous plants may be, and supervise his explorations.

WELCOMING THE MINI SCHNAUZER

Overview

- Before bringing your puppy home, you should have purchased all of the necessary accessories and done a complete safety check on your home, removing all possible puppy dangers.
- Among the items you will need are puppy food, food and water bowls, a leash and collar and a dog crate.
- Let your pup take it easy for the first couple of days. He has just made a big change and needs time to adjust without being overwhelmed.
- Make all introductions carefully and under supervision, especially where children and other pets are concerned.
- Take your breeder's advice about choosing a good-quality puppy food.

House-training the Mini Schnauzer

Every Miniature Schnauzer puppy deserves a room of his own, a safe and cozy harbor where he can feel secure. I know what you're thinking…and no, a crate is not cruel, nor is it punishment for your pup. Canines are natural den creatures, thanks to the thousands of years their ancestors spent living in caves and cavities in the ground. Therefore, pups adapt quite naturally to crate confinement.

Training your Miniature Schnauzer that the outdoors is the place to relieve himself is a major component in your happy life together.

Puppies are also inherently clean and hate to soil their "dens" or living spaces, which makes the crate a natural house-training aid. Thus his crate is actually a multi-purpose dog accessory—your Miniature Schnauzer's personal doghouse within your house, a humane house-training tool, a security measure that will protect your household and antique furniture when you're not home, a travel aid to house and protect your dog when traveling (most motels will accept a crated dog) and, finally, a comfy dog space for your puppy when your anti-dog relatives come to visit.

Some experienced breeders insist on crate use after their puppies leave, and a few even crate-train their pups to some extent before they send them home. But it's more likely that your Miniature Schnauzer pup has never seen a crate, so it's up to you to make sure his introduction to his crate is a pleasant one.

Everyone in the family can help with the Mini Schnauzer puppy's house-training. Puppies need to go out very often, so it will be helpful to have several family members split up the "shifts."

Crate use is a wonderful tool for house-training and beyond. For example, at many shows the dogs wait in their crates when it's not their turn in the ring.

Miniature Schnauzer

When first introducing your Miniature Schnauzer to his crate, toss a tiny treat into the crate to entice him to go in and continue doing so for the first day or two. Pick a crate command, such as "Kennel," "Inside" or "Crate," and use it when he enters. Introduce the crate as soon as he comes home so he learns that this is his new "house." You also can feed his first few meals inside the crate with the door still open so that the crate association will be a happy one.

The puppy should sleep in his crate beginning on his very first night home. He may whine or object to the confinement, but be strong and stay the course. If you release him when he cries, you provide his first life lesson…if I cry, I get out and maybe even hugged. Not a good lesson to teach him.

A better scheme is to place the crate next to your bed at night for the first few weeks. Your presence will comfort him, and you'll also know if he needs a middle-of-the-night potty trip. Whatever you do, do not lend comfort by taking the puppy into bed with you. To a dog, on the bed means equal, which is not a good idea this early on, when you are trying to establish yourself as the leader.

Make a practice of placing the puppy in his crate for naps, at nighttime and whenever you are unable to watch him closely. Not to worry…he will let you know when he wakes up and needs a potty trip. If he falls asleep under the table and wakes up when you're not there, guess what he'll do first? Make a puddle, then toddle over to say "Hi!"

Become a Miniature Schnauzer vigilante. Routines, consistency and an eagle eye are your keys to house-training success. Puppies always "go" when they wake up (quickly now!), after eating, after play periods and after brief periods of confinement. Most pups under 12 weeks of age will need to eliminate at least every hour or so, which can be 10 or more times a day (set your oven timer to remind you). Always take puppy outside to the same area, telling him "Outside" as you go out. Pick a "potty" cue, ("Hurry up," "Go potty" and "Get busy" are the most popular), and use it when he does his business, lavishing him with "Good puppy!" praise. Always use the same exit door for these potty trips, and confine puppy to the exit area so he can find it when he needs it. Watch for sniffing and circling, sure signs he needs to relieve himself. Don't allow him to roam the house until he's house-trained…how will he find that outside door if he's three or four rooms away? He's not that familiar with the layout of the house yet.

Of course, he will have accidents. All puppies do. If you catch him in the act, clap your hands loudly, say "Aaah! Aaah!" and scoop him up to go outside. Your voice should startle him and make him stop. Be sure to praise him when he finishes his duty outside.

If you discover the piddle spot after the fact…more than three or four seconds later…you're too late. All dogs only understand *in the moment*

Crating your Mini Schnauzer when traveling helps keep him safe in the car while encouraging him to "hold it" until you make a rest stop.

and will not understand a correction given more than five seconds (that's only *five*) after the deed. Correcting any later will only cause fear, confusion and possible aberrant behavior. Just forget it and vow to be more vigilant.

Never (that is spelled *n-e-v-e-r*) rub your puppy's nose in his mistake or strike your puppy or adult dog with your hand, a newspaper or another object to correct him or for any other reason. He will not understand and will only become fearful of the person who is hitting or abusing him.

Here's a house-training hint: remove puppy's water after 7 p.m. to aid in nighttime bladder control. If he gets thirsty, offer him an ice cube. Then just watch him race for the refrigerator when he hears the rattle of the ice-cube tray.

Despite its many benefits, crate use can be abused. Puppies under 12 weeks of age should never be confined for more than two hours at a time, unless, of course, they are sleeping. A general rule of thumb is three hours maximum for a three-month-old pup, four hours for a four- to five-month-old, and no more than six hours for dogs over six months of age. If you're unable to be home to release the dog, arrange for a relative, neighbor or dog-sitter to let him out to exercise and potty.

If you are unable to use a crate for house-training, or prefer to paper-train your Mini Schnauzer puppy, the routine is basically the same. Sometimes this is the only option for city dogs. Assign an out-of-the-way elimination place and cover it with newspaper. Take your puppy to the designated papered area on schedule. Use the specified potty word, and praise when he does his business. Do not use the area for any other purpose except potty breaks. Keep the area clean. You can place a small piece of soiled paper on the clean ones to remind puppy why he's there. His nose will tell him what to do.

What to do with an uncrated puppy when you're not home? Confine him to one area with a dog-proof barrier. Puppy proofing alone won't be enough protection even in a stripped environment…a bored Miniature Schnauzer pup may chew through drywall. An exercise pen, 4 feet by 4 feet square (available through pet suppliers) and sturdy enough that pup can't knock it down, will provide safe containment for short periods. Paper one area for elimination, with perhaps a blanket in the opposite corner for napping. Miniature Schnauzer puppies are seldom content to just lie around chomping on a chew toy. If you don't or won't crate-train and cannot supervise your pup, be prepared to meet the consequences.

Most importantly, remember that successful house-training revolves around consistency and repetition. Maintain a strict schedule and use your key words consistently. Well-trained owners have well-trained Miniature Schnauzer pups.

HOUSE-TRAINING THE MINI SCHNAUZER

Overview

- The first type of training you will do with your Mini Schnauzer puppy is teaching him proper toileting habits. This is the key to clean living with your dog.
- Crates are not cruel! A crate is a most helpful tool for your pup's house-training and safety; it has a multitude of uses.
- The crate must be your pup's happy place where he feels secure. Never use it as a form of punishment.
- Be vigilant in taking your pup to his relief area often and watching for signs that he needs to relieve himself.
- Only scold your pup for potty accidents if you catch him *in the act*. Likewise, praise him while in the act when he goes in the right spot.
- Paper training may be an option for some Miniature Schnauzer owners.

Puppy Pre-School

If you want to live in harmony with your Miniature Schnauzer, you have to be the top dog in his life. The Miniature Schnauzer, albeit small, is a strong and sturdy dog that is infamous for his stubborn streak; so early training is especially important for a Miniature Schnauzer. Puppy kindergarten should start on the day you bring your puppy home.

Before your puppy left his breeder, all of his life lessons came from his mom and littermates. When he

Your Miniature Schnauzer pup makes a bright and eager student, quick to learn when his considerable puppy energy is focused on you.

played too rough or nipped too hard, his siblings cried and stopped the game. When he got pushy or obnoxious, his mother cuffed him gently with a maternal paw. Now his human family has to communicate appropriate behavior in terms that his young canine mind will understand. Remember, too, that from a canine perspective human rules make no sense at all.

Getting your pup accustomed to his collar and lead, and getting his attention with things like toys and treats, are precursors to teaching him the basic commands.

When you start the teaching process, keep this thought uppermost: the first 20 weeks of any canine's life is the most valuable learning time, a period when his mind is best able to soak up every lesson, both positive and negative. Positive experiences and proper socialization during this period are critical to his future development and stability. We'll learn more about socialization later, but know this: the amount and quality of time you invest with your youngster now will

At 16 weeks of age, this Mini Schnauzer youngster is still in the prime of his "sponge" stage, ready to soak up whatever you can teach him.

determine what kind of an adult he will become. Wild dog or gentleman or lady? Well-behaved or naughty dog? It's up to you.

Canine research tells us that any behavior that is rewarded (called positive reinforcement) will be repeated. If something good happens, like a tasty treat or hugs and kisses, the puppy will naturally want to repeat the behavior. Canine behavioral science also has proven that one of the best ways to a puppy's mind is through his stomach. Never underestimate the power of liver! This leads to a very important puppy rule: keep your pockets loaded with puppy treats at all times, so you are prepared to reinforce good behavior whenever it occurs.

That same reinforcement principle also applies to negative behavior, or what we humans might consider negative (like digging in the trash can, which the dog or puppy does not know is "wrong"). If pup gets into the garbage, steals food or does anything else that makes him feel good, he will do it again. What better reason to keep a sharp eye on your puppy to prevent those "normal" canine behaviors?

You are about to begin Puppy Class 101. Rule number one: puppy must learn that you are now the "alpha" dog and his new pack leader. Rule number two: you have to teach him in a manner he will understand (sorry, barking just won't do it). Remember always that your Mini Schnauzer knows nothing about human standards of behavior.

WORD ASSOCIATION
Use the same word (command) for each behavior every time you teach it, adding food rewards and

verbal praise to reinforce the positive behavior. The pup will make the connection and will be motivated to repeat the action when he hears those key words. For example, when teaching the

he eliminates, adding a "Good boy!" while he's urinating or emptying his bowels. Your Miniature Schnauzer pup will soon learn what those trips outside are for.

A pup's siblings are his first "classmates," as he learns many valuable life lessons from his mother and through interacting with the other pups in the litter.

pup to potty outside, use the same potty term ("Go potty," "Get busy" or "Hurry up" are commonly used) each time

TIMING

All dogs learn their lessons in the present tense. You have to catch them in the act (good or bad) in order to dispense rewards or discipline. You have three to five seconds to connect with him or he will not understand what he did wrong. Thus timing and consistency are your keys to success in teaching any new behavior or correcting bad behaviors.

PUPPY TRAINING PRINCIPLES
Successful puppy training depends on several important principles:

1. Use simple one-word commands and say them only once. Otherwise puppy learns that "Come" (or "Sit" or "Down") is a three- or four-word command.
2. Never correct your dog for something he did minutes earlier. You have three to five seconds to catch him. Be on your toes—puppies commit crimes quickly.
3. Always praise (and offer a treat) as soon as he does something good (or stops doing something naughty). How else will puppy know he's a good dog?
4. Be consistent. You can't snuggle together on the couch to watch TV today, then scold him for climbing on the couch tomorrow.
5. Never tell your dog to come to you and then correct him for something he did wrong. He will think the correction is for coming to you. (Think like a dog, remember?) Always go to the dog to stop unwanted behavior, but be sure you catch him in the act.
6. Never hit or kick your dog or strike him with a newspaper or another object. Such physical abuse will only create fear and confusion in your dog and could provoke aggressive

behavior down the road.
7. When praising or correcting, use your best doggie voice. Use a light your puppy feel like he's been a good fellow.

Your dog also will respond accordingly to

Start teaching your pup to come to you by enticing him with a favorite toy. You always want his coming to you to result in something good for him; that way, he will be eager to respond every time you call.

and happy voice for praise, and a firm, sharp voice for warnings or corrections. A whiny "No, No" or "Drop that" will not sound too convincing, nor will a deep, gruff voice make family arguments. If there's a shouting match, he will think that he did something wrong and head for cover. So never argue in front of the kids...*or* the dog!

Despite the Miniature Schnauzer's sometimes

stubborn nature, he is a soft dog who will not respond to harsh training methods or corrections. Puppy kindergarten and continued lessons in obedience focusing on positive reinforcement are the best course to combating the Miniature Schnauzer stubborn streak.

GAMES WITH YOUR PUPPY
Puppy games are a great way to entertain your puppy and yourself while subliminally teaching lessons in the course of having fun. Start with a game plan and a pocketful of tasty dog treats. Keep your games short so you don't push his attention span beyond Miniature Schnauzer puppy limits. Mini Schnauzers get bored with too much repetition.

"Puppy catch-me" is a game that helps to teach the come command. With two people sitting on the floor about 10 or 15 feet apart, one person holds and pets the pup while the other calls him: "Puppy, puppy, come!" in a happy voice. When the puppy comes running, lavish big hugs on him and give a tasty treat. Repeat back and forth several times...don't overdo it.

You can add a ball or toy and toss it back and forth for the puppy to retrieve. When he picks it up, praise and hug some more, give him a goodie to release the toy, then toss it back to person number two. Repeat as before.

Hide-and-seek also teaches the come command. Play this game outdoors in your yard or other confined safe area. When the pup is distracted, hide behind a tree or bush. Peek out to see when he discovers you are gone and comes running back to find you (trust me, he will do that). As soon as he gets close, come out, squat down with arms outstretched and call him: "Puppy, come!" This is also an excellent bonding aid and teaches the puppy to depend on you.

"Where's your toy?" is an ideal beginner retrieving game. Begin by placing one of his favorite toys in plain sight, ask your puppy "Where's your toy?" and let him take it. Then place your puppy safely outside the room and place the toy so that only part of it shows. Bring him back and ask the same question. Praise highly when he finds it. Repeat several times. Finally, conceal the toy completely and let your puppy sniff it out. Trust his nose...he will find his toy.

Miniature Schnauzer puppies love to have fun with their people. Games are excellent teaching aids, and one of the best ways to teach the puppy trust and obedience.

PUPPY PRE-SCHOOL

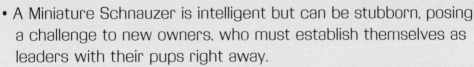

Overview

- A Miniature Schnauzer is intelligent but can be stubborn, posing a challenge to new owners, who must establish themselves as leaders with their pups right away.
- Take advantage of your pup's capacity to learn when young. Start training him as soon as he comes home.
- Positive reinforcement is the preferred way of training dogs. It definitely is the best way to train a Miniature Schnauzer.
- Word association and timing are two essential components of training success.
- Learn and practice the basic principles of training a dog.
- Introduce commands through play. Games will encourage your Mini Schnauzer to come to you, and he will associate it with fun.

Teaching Basic Commands

Start your puppy's lessons as soon as he comes home. Research has proven that the earlier you begin, the easier the process and the more successful you both will be.

Always start your teaching exercises in a quiet, distraction-free environment. Once your Miniature Schnauzer pup has mastered any task, change the setting and practice in a different location, like another room or the yard, and then practice with another person or a dog nearby. If the pup reacts to the new distraction and does not perform the exercise, back up

Your training efforts will pay off in a well-mannered Miniature Schnauzer whose intelligence and sparkling personality you can fully appreciate and enjoy.

and continue with the exercise by going back to practicing with no distractions for a while.

Appoint one person to instruct your puppy in the early stages so that your pup is not confused. It's the "too-many-cooks" rule of dog training. Once the puppy has learned a command reliably, other family members can join in.

Ignore your Miniature Schnauzer for a few minutes before each training session (just a few minutes, as Miniature Schnauzers do not like to be ignored). The lack of stimulation will make him more eager for your company and attention.

Keep lessons short so your puppy won't get bored or lose his enthusiasm. This is especially important with a Miniature Schnauzer. In time, he will be able to concentrate for longer periods. Vary the exercises to keep his enthusiasm level high. Watch for signs of boredom and loss of attention.

A polite sit by the owner's side is the starting point for many exercises. For that reason, and because the exercise is relatively simple, the sit is often the first exercise taught.

The down/stay is a challenging exercise to teach, especially to a breed with a streak of terrier independence. As dogs view the down as a submissive posture, it is rarely a favorite position to assume.

Always keep your training sessions positive and upbeat. Use lots of praise, praise and more praise. Never train your puppy or adult dog if you are in a grumpy mood. You will lose patience, and he will think it is his fault, which will reverse any progress the two of you have made.

Finish every training session on a positive note. If you have been struggling or unsuccessful, switch gears and do something he knows well (sit!) and end the session.

EARLY LESSON PLANS

Before you can effectively teach your puppy any command, two things must happen. Your puppy must learn to respond to his name (name recognition), and you must be able to gain and hold his attention. How to accomplish that? Why, with treats, of course. Most Miniature Schnauzers live for food!

Treats are defined as tiny tidbits, preferably soft and easy to chew. You don't want to overfeed the pup. Thin slices of hotdogs cut in quarters work well.

Attention and Name Recognition

Start by calling your Miniature Schnauzer puppy's name. Once. Not two or three times, but once. Otherwise, he will learn he has a three-part name and will ignore you when you say it once. Begin by using his name when he is undistracted and you know that he will look at you. Pop him a tiny piece of a treat as soon as he looks at you. Repeat this at least a dozen times, several times a day. It won't take more than a day or so before he understands that his name means something good to eat.

Establish a Release Command

Your release command is what you'll use to tell him that the exercise is over, similar to "At ease" in the military. "All done" and "Free" are the ones most commonly recommended. You'll need a release command so your Miniature Schnauzer will know that it's okay to relax or move from a stationary position.

Take It and Leave It

These commands offer too many advantages to list. Place a treat in the palm of your hand and tell your pup to "Take it" as he grabs the treat. Repeat three times. On the fourth time, do not say a word when your pup reaches for the treat…just close your fingers around the treat and wait. Do not pull away, but be prepared for the pup to paw, lick, bark and nibble on your fingers. When he finally pulls away from your hand, usually in puzzlement, open your hand and tell him "Take it."

Now, the next step. Show your Miniature Schnauzer the treat in the palm of your hand and tell him to "Leave it." When he goes for the treat, close your hand and repeat

"Leave it." Repeat the process until he pulls away, wait just a second, then open your hand and tell him to "Take it." Repeat "Leave it" until he waits

A Miniature Schnauzer may need some extra encouragement to assume the down position, so be as positive and persuasive as you can!

just a few seconds, then give the treat on "Take it." Gradually extend the time you wait when he leaves it on command, and before you tell him "Take it."

Now you want to teach your dog to leave things on the ground, not just in your hand (think of all the things you don't want him to pick up).

Position yourself in front of your dog and toss a treat behind you and a little to the side, so he can see the treat, and tell him to "Leave it." Here begins the dance. If he goes for the treat, use your body, not your hands, to block him, moving him backwards away from it. As soon as he backs off and gives up trying to get around you, unblock the treat and tell him "Take it." Be ready to block again if he goes for it before you give permission. Repeat the process until he understands and waits for the command.

Once your Miniature Schnauzer knows this well, practice with his food dish, telling him to "Leave it," then "Take it" after he complies (he can either sit or stand while waiting for his dish). As before, gradually extend the waiting period before you tell him to "Take it."

This little training exercise sends many messages to your Miniature Schnauzer. He is reminded that you're the boss, that all good things, like food, come from his master. It will help prevent your puppy from becoming too possessive of his food bowl, a behavior that only escalates and leads to more serious aggressive behaviors. The benefits of a solid "Take it/Leave it" are endless.

BASIC EXERCISES

Come Command
This command has life-saving potential...preventing your Mini Schnauzer from getting away from you, running into the street, going after a squirrel, chasing a child on a bike... the list goes on and on.

Always practice this command on leash. You can't afford to risk failure or your pup will learn that he does not always have to come when called, and you want him to respond reliably to your call. Once you have the pup's attention, call him from a short distance with "Puppy, Come!" (use your happy voice) and give a treat when he comes to you. If he hesitates, tug him to you gently with his leash. Grasp and hold his collar with one hand as you dispense the treat. This is important. You will eventually phase out the treat and switch to hands-on praise. This maneuver also connects holding his collar with coming and treating, which will assist you in countless future behaviors.

Do 10 or 12 repetitions, 2 or 3 times a day. Once your pup has mastered the come command, continue to practice daily to engrave this most important behavior into his brain. Experienced Miniature Schnauzer owners know, however, that you can never completely trust a dog to come when called if the dog is bent on a self-appointed mission. "Off leash" is often synonymous with "out of control," which is dangerous for the dog.

Sit Command

This one's a snap, since your Miniature Schnauzer already understands the treating process. Stand in front of your pup, move the treat directly over his nose and slowly move it backwards. As he folds backwards to reach the goodie, his rear will move downward to the floor. If the puppy raises up to reach the treat, just lower it a bit. The moment his behind touches the floor, tell him "Sit." (That's one word…"Sit.") Release the treat and gently grasp that collar as you did with "Come." He will again make that positive

Training is most effective when based on positive reinforcement, consistency and trust.

connection between the treat, the sit position and the collar hold.

As time goes by, make him hold the sit position longer before you treat (this is the beginning of the stay command). Start using your release word to release him

Is your Mini Schnauzer a retriever in disguise? Use games of fetch to encourage the dog to return to you, thus reinforcing the come command.

from the sit position. Practice using the sit command for everyday activities, such as sitting for his food bowl or a toy. Do random sits throughout the day, always for a food or praise reward. Once he is reliable, combine the "Sit" and "Leave it" for his food dish. Your pup is expanding his vocabulary.

Stay Command

"Stay" is really just an extension of "Sit," which your Miniature Schnauzer already knows. With the puppy sitting when commanded, place the palm of your hand in front of his nose and tell him "Stay." Count to five. Give him his release word to leave the stay position and then praise him.

Stretch out the stays in tiny increments, making allowances for puppy energy. Once he stays reliably, take one step backward, then forward again. Gradually extend the time and distance that you move away. If the puppy moves from his stay position, say "No" and move forward in front of him. Use sensible timelines depending on your puppy's attention span.

Down Command

The down can be a tough command to master. Because the down is a submissive posture, take-charge breeds like the Mini Schnauzer may find it especially difficult. That's why it's most important to teach it to your pup when he is very young.

From the sit position, move the food lure from his nose to the ground and slightly backward between his front paws. Wiggle it as necessary. As soon as his front legs and rear end hit the floor, give him the treat and tell him "Down, Good boy, down" thus connecting the word to the behavior. Be patient and be generous with the praise when he cooperates.

Once he goes into the down position with ease, incorporate the stay command as you did with sit. By six months of age, the puppy should be able to do a solid sit/stay for ten minutes, ditto for a down/stay.

Heel Command

The actual heel command comes a bit later in the learning curve. A young Miniature Schnauzer should

Teaching your puppy how to walk nicely on lead will progress to the formal heel command when he is older.

be taught simply to walk politely on a leash, at or near your side. That is best accomplished when your pup is very young and small, before he tries to pull you down the street—he's small, but strong!

Start leash training as soon as your pup comes home. Simply attach the leash to his buckle collar and let him drag the leash around for a little while every day. If he chews his leash, distract him with play activities or spray the leash with a product made to deter chewing, which will make it taste unpleasant. Play a game with the leash on.

After a few days, gather up the leash in a distraction-free zone of the house or yard and take just a few steps together. Hold a treat lure at your side

There's not much chance of your diminutive Mini Schnauzer's dragging you down the street, but he must be well-behaved on lead nonetheless.

to encourage the puppy to walk next to you. Pat your knee and use a happy voice. Move forward just a few steps each time. Say "Let's go!" when you move forward, hold the treat to keep him near, take a few steps, give the treat and give him lots of praise!

Keep these sessions short and happy, a mere 30 seconds at a time. Never scold or nag him into walking faster or slower; just encourage him with happy talk. Walk straight ahead at first, adding wide turns once he gets the hang of it. Progress to 90° turns, using a gentle leash tug, a happy verbal "Let's go!" and, of course, a treat. Walk in short 30- to 40-second bursts, with a happy break (use your release word) and brief play (hugs will do nicely) in between. Keep total training time short and always quit with success, even if just a few short steps.

Wait Command

You'll love this one, especially when your Miniature Schnauzer comes into the house with wet or muddy paws. Work on the wait command with a closed door. Start to open the door as if to go through or out. When your dog tries to follow, step in front and body-block him to prevent his passage. Don't use the wait command just yet. Keep it up until he gives up and you can open the door a little to pass through. Then say "Through" or "Okay" and let him go through the door. Repeat by body-blocking until he understands and waits for you, then start applying the word "Wait" to the behavior. Practice in different doorways inside your home, using outside entrances (to safe or enclosed areas) only after he will wait reliably.

KEEP PRACTICING

Ongoing practice in obedience is actually a lifetime dog rule, especially for a strong-willed Miniature Schnauzer. Dogs will be dogs, and, if we don't maintain their skills, they will sink back into sloppy, inattentive behaviors that will be harder to correct. Incorporate these commands into your daily routine and your dog will remain a Mini of whom you can be proud.

TEACHING BASIC COMMANDS

Overview

- Begin lessons in a distraction-free environment, keeping lessons short so that your puppy doesn't lose focus or become bored.
- Training time should be happy time. Don't train your pup if you are in a bad mood, and remember to keep things positive.
- Before beginning the basic commands, your pup must recognize his name and you must be able to hold his attention.
- "Take it" and "Leave it" are important to teach, along with a release word to let the puppy know when an exercise is over.
- Basic exercises include sit, down, stay, come and heel.
- Practice should be ongoing throughout your Mini Schnauzer's life so that he maintains a keen knowledge of the commands.

Feeding the Mini Schnauzer

Feeding your dog is like putting gasoline into your car. You can't use a poor-quality product and expect maximum performance or results. A quality dog food is the best route to your Miniature Schnauzer's overall health. The less expensive foods do not provide a fully digestible product, nor do they contain a proper balance of the vitamins, minerals and fatty acids that are necessary to support healthy muscle, tissue, skin and coat. Canine nutrition research has proven that you have to feed larger quantities of a

The best food for the first few weeks of any puppy's life doesn't come from a bag or a can, but from his mother.

cheaper food to maintain proper body weight.

Premium dog-food manufacturers have developed their formulas with strict quality controls, using only quality ingredients obtained from reliable sources. The labels on the food bags tell you what ingredients are in the food (beef, chicken, corn, etc.), with the ingredients listed in descending order of weight or amount in the food. Do not add your own supplements, "people food" or extra vitamins to the food. Certain foods, like chocolate, onions, grapes, raisins and nuts, are actually toxic to dogs. Plus, you will upset the nutritional balance of the dog food by adding extras, which could affect the growth pattern of your Miniature Schnauzer pup or maintenance of your adult.

In the world of quality dog foods, there are enough choices to confuse even experienced dog folks. The

Feeding the pup can be a family affair. A puppy should always accept his food in a friendly manner, never snapping or showing other signs of food-aggression.

When you travel, don't forget your Mini Schnauzer's food and some water for the trip. Crates often have bowls that attach to the inside, making eating and drinking convenient for the pooch on the go.

major dog-food manufacturers now offer formulas for every breed, age and activity level. The new "growth" foods contain protein and fat levels that are appropriate for the different-sized breeds. For example, large, fast-growing breeds require less protein and fat during their early months of rapid growth, which is better for healthy joint development. Accordingly, medium and small (like your Miniature Schnauzer) breeds also have different nutritional requirements during their first year of growth. Ask your breeder and your vet what food they recommend for your Miniature Schnauzer's critical first year.

Don't be intimidated by all of those dog-food bags on the store shelves. Read the labels on the bags (how else can you learn what's in those foods?) and call the information numbers on the dog-food bags. A solid education in the dog-food business, along with advice from your vet and breeder, will provide the tools you need to offer your dog a diet that is best for his long-term health.

As with human infants, puppies require a diet different from that of an adult. If you plan to switch from the food fed by your breeder, take home a small supply of the breeder's food to mix with your own to aid your puppy's adjustment to his new food.

When and how much to feed? An eight-week-old puppy does best eating three times a day. (Tiny tummies, tiny meals.) As he gets older, you can switch to twice-daily feeding. Most breeders suggest two meals a day for the life of the dog, regardless of the breed, as this is healthier for dogs' digestion than one large daily meal.

Free feeding is not recommended. Free feeding fosters picky eating habits...a bite here, a nibble there. Free feeders also are more likely to become possessive of their food bowls, a problem behavior that signals the beginning of resource guarding and aggression. Scheduled meals give you one more opportunity to remind your Miniature Schnauzer that all good things in life come from you, his owner and pack leader.

With scheduled meals, it's also easier to predict elimination, which is the better road to house-training. Regular meals help you know just how much the puppy eats and when, valuable information that will allow you to recognize changes in his appetite, which could be indicative of a health problem.

Like people, puppies and adult dogs have different appetites; some will lick their food bowls clean and beg for more, while others pick at their food and leave some of it untouched. It's easy to overfeed a "chow-hound." Who can resist those pleading Miniature Schnauzer eyes? Be strong and stay the right course. Chubby puppies may be cute and cuddly, but the extra weight will stress growing joints and is thought to be a factor in the development of skeletal problems like hip and elbow disease or knee problems. Overweight pups also tend to grow into overweight adults who tire easily and will be more susceptible to other health problems.

So always remember that lean is healthy, fat is not. Obesity is a major canine killer. Quite simply, a lean dog lives longer than one who is overweight. And that doesn't even reflect the better quality of life for the lean dog that can run, jump and play without the burden of an extra 5 or 10 pounds.

Mealtime can be a time to reinforce commands and your Mini's polite behavior. Dogs should always wait for their owners' OK before eating, never jumping up or grabbing to get at their food bowls.

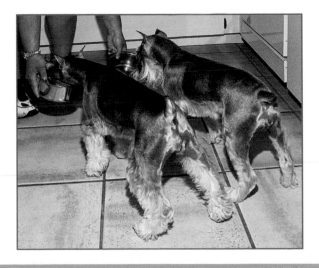

Should you feed canned or dry food? If you choose dry food, should you offer it with or without water? Dry food is recommended by most vets, since the dry particles help clean the dog's teeth of plaque and tartar. Adding water to dry food is optional. The food hog who almost inhales his food may do better with a splash of water in his food pan to encourage him to eat more slowly. A bit of water added immediately before eating is also thought to enhance the flavor of the food while still preserving the dental benefits. Whether feeding wet or dry, always have water available at all times.

To complicate the dog-food dilemma, there are also raw-food diets for those who prefer to feed their dogs a completely natural diet rather than traditional manufactured dog food. The debate on raw and/or all-natural versus manufactured is a fierce one, with the raw proponents claiming that raw-food diets have cured their dogs' allergies and other chronic ailments. If you are interested in this alternative feeding method, there are several books on raw diets written by nutrition experts. You can also check with your vet, ask your breeder and surf the Internet.

If your adult dog is overweight (you should be able to see a "waistline" when viewing your dog from above and see a "tuck-up" in the abdominal area from the side), you can switch to a "light" food, which has fewer calories and more fiber. "Senior" foods for older dogs have formulas

A high-quality balanced diet will be evident in the dog's overall health and activity level, and in a shiny vibrant coat like this striking black and silver Mini's.

designed to meet the needs of less active older dogs. "Performance" diets contain more fat and protein for dogs that work, compete in sporting disciplines or lead very active lives. The bottom line is this: what and how much you feed your dog is a major factor in his overall health and longevity. It's worth your investment in extra time and dollars to provide the best diet for your dog. You are advised to check out the dog-food aisle at your local pet-supply store. Grocery stores don't usually have the selection of premium-quality foods that the pet-supply stores will offer. Pet shops only sell the better dog foods, as these are recommended by top breeders and vets.

FEEDING THE MINI SCHNAUZER

Overview

- The easiest way to give your Mini Schnauzer the nutrition he needs is by feeding him a food designed to be complete and balanced for his stage of life.
- Supplementation, feeding extras and offering "people food" can be harmful to your dog as well as upset the balance of his diet.
- Puppy foods are formulated for healthy growth. You can continue feeding your puppy what the breeder had been giving him.
- Scheduled feeding is best throughout the dog's life for many reasons, including house-training purposes and for you to know how much your dog is eating.
- Obesity can cause illness, skeletal problems and even death in dogs. Proper feeding is about maintaining healthy weight just as it is about proper nutrition.
- Your breeder and vet are trusted sources of advice about feeding your Miniature Schnauzer.

CHAPTER 11

Grooming the Mini Schnauzer

Grooming the Miniature Schnauzer for the show ring is an art that takes practice. The Mini Schnauzer's coat, like that of a terrier, must be hand-stripped to maintain proper hard texture.

T he outline of the Miniature Schnauzer is unmistakable. Trimmed in his Sunday show best, this bearded fellow possesses elegant lines, a wiry topcoat and well-fringed column-like legs. Like those of the terrier breeds, the Miniature Schnauzer's coat must be hand-stripped to achieve the correct harsh texture. Hand-stripping involves the plucking of dead coat to keep the coat wiry and harsh. Of course, pet owners need not worry about learning how to hand-strip their Minis, though clippering is required to keep the dog's outline correct.

Grooming the Miniature Schnauzer exacts an owner's commitment; although the coat doesn't grow as full as that of a Poodle, for example, it does grow continually and need attention on a regular basis. You have selected this breed because you like its physical and temperamental attributes, and the breed's distinctive coat is one of its hallmarks. To not trim the dog properly would do an injustice to the breed. It's important for your Miniature Schnauzer to look like a Miniature Schnauzer. To be sure, an ungroomed Mini doesn't really look like anything special, and there's never been a Mini who wasn't special!

Show grooming is an art that requires specialized skills and abilities. If you plan to show your Mini, arrange for lessons with an experienced handler or groomer.

Your commitment to grooming your Mini includes a daily once-over with a slicker brush. Do not brush too hard into the dog's skin as it can cause irritation. Once or twice a week, you should brush the facial and leg furnishings to keep them from matting.

How much and the type of grooming equipment you will need depends on if you intend to maintain your Mini Schnauzer in show coat or pet trim.

The ears require a little attention weekly as well. Remove any hairs growing inside the ear canal, as these can cause problems if left to grow downward into the canal. Ear powder makes the hairs easier to grasp, and many groomers use a tweezers or hemostat to remove the hairs. Apply some lotion on a cotton wipe to remove the powder after you've plucked out the hair. Always check for any accumulation of wax or dirt in the ear. An ear-cleansing solution will help keep the ears clean and fresh-smelling.

The coat of the Miniature Schnauzer is a double coat, with a hard and wiry outercoat and a soft, dense undercoat. Of course, all dogs shed. Although the Mini's coat only blows twice a year (perhaps more for bitches in season), small black hairs fall onto the carpet every day. Since the Mini is mini, there's not that much coat, but there is some. During the shedding season, it's the soft white coat that billows around the house, not the dark outer hairs.

Only experienced breeders and show groomers really know how to hand-strip the Miniature Schnauzer. It's an art that requires practice, technique and much patience. A show Mini must be a well-trained and very patient creature to endure the process. When done properly, it is pain-free for the dog. If you are serious about learning how to hand-strip your dog, you should visit a dog show to talk to handlers. One-on-one lessons are the best way to learn this technique.

Although the pet Mini, trimmed with an electric clipper, will never have the nice harsh coat of a show dog, he still will have the correct Miniature Schnauzer outline. The topcoat disappears when the dog is clippered. Nonetheless, he will look neat and trimmed and be a pleasure to have around.

Most pet owners rely upon a grooming salon to trim their Miniature Schnauzers. You can make the appointment coincide with your own hair salon visit, about once every five or six weeks. Professional groomers can be costly, so many owners opt to take on the task themselves. If you think you would like to learn how to trim your Mini at home, then let's look at this more closely. The American Miniature Schnauzer Club provides excellent guidelines and diagrams, and owners can visit them at http://amsc.us.

BRUSHES, COMBS AND MORE

Purchase the best-quality grooming tools from a pet-supply store or a good online catalog. You'll need a pin brush (straight metal pins in a rubber cushion), a slicker brush (short metal pins with curved ends), a greyhound comb (combination of fine and medium spaced teeth), a high-quality pair of scissors (sharp!), thinning shears (single blade with 42 to 46 teeth), and a nail clipper or grinder. For the electric clipper, you will want to purchase a name-brand device with detachable blades. You're saving money by not

going to the salon, spend some of it on your clipper. You should buy five blades: #10, #30, #40, #7F and #15. The higher the number the closer it will cut the hair. Don't forget to buy oil for the clipper, too. Now for the furniture: the grooming table. This investment will save you money at the chiropractor's office, as it saves your back from hours of stress. You can buy a sturdy grooming table with an arm (or hanger) and noose with a non-slip surface (usually a rubber mat). You place the dog

Make your puppy's pedicures as pleasant as possible. Be comforting and reassuring, holding him gently as you clip.

on the grooming table with his head through the noose. The table should have an adjustable height, which makes it convenient for you and comfortable for your back.

Before you can plop your Mini on the table and turn on the clipper: wait a minute (or a week!). You must train the dog to stand on the table. Minis don't naturally just stand on a table with a noose around their neck and feel calm. The stand/stay command reinforces to the dog that he is not to move, jump, stand up or otherwise carry on. Whether or not you are doing the grooming yourself, you still will have to train your Mini to stand/stay. Your groomer will appreciate your efforts to train your dog. After a few lessons, the dog will understand that he is expected to remain in a stand/stay while he's being groomed.

First we brush. Take the pin brush and give the dog a thorough once-over, including his leg furnishings, his beard and underskirt. Work through any mats gently, without pulling on the dog's skin. Once a mat is wet, it becomes virtually detangle-proof. Line-brushing is the term used for upward brushing strokes (against the lay of the hair), beginning at the top of the leg and downward. After you have brushed through all of the furnishings as well as the underarms and toes, take your greyhound comb and slowly comb through the coat to ensure that there are no knots or mats. If your dog has a really dense, full coat, you will want to use the slicker brush for the first brushing.

BATH TIME

The dog is now ready for a bath—not the favorite activity of any Mini. Introducing the puppy to the bathing process early on will be time well spent. A stubborn Mini fighting you in the sink never makes a pretty picture. Now that the dog is tangle-free, you can begin bathing him in a basin or large sink. Do not use human soap products on your dog. There are many superior doggy shampoos on the market, and any one of these will work fine. We recommend that you dilute the shampoo with water before applying it to the dog's coat. Use warm water, never hot. Work the shampoo into the dog's coat, but do not rub it in on his furnishings or you will cause tangles.

You may wish to insert cotton balls into the dog's ears to prevent water from getting inside the ear canal. Don't forget to remove them when you're done, or you'll think that you've washed away your dog's training along with his dirt. Use common sense when bathing the dog: keep the water away from his eyes. If you make bathing enjoyable, your Mini will be more cooperative. If you spray him in the face, scald him with hot water and half-drown him in the process of removing the last soap sud, who would blame him from running from you the next time you take out that scary

basin! On a serious note, be sure that you get all of the soap out of the coat, as residue can cause irritation, dryness or flaking.

Drying, of course, requires a blow dryer and lots of towels. When taking the dog out of the sink or basin, be quick to entowel him in soft terry cloth. He will naturally want to shake out the water from his coat, which effectively will be your shower for the day no doubt. You will use a towel on the furnishings to squeeze out the excess water—don't rub or you'll cause tangles. With the hand-held dryer, blow the coat while brushing with the pin brush. When drying the legs, brush upwards and blow the hair straight until it's completely dry.

With a breed like the Miniature Schnauzer, which requires considerable grooming, training your Miniature Schnauzer to stand on a grooming table will make the task much easier for both of you.

For the beard and other facial furnishings, brush down. Do not use a slicker brush on the coat until it is completely dry, as it can pull out the coat, especially on the legs.

ENTER THE BARBER

You are not only your Miniature Schnauzer's pal, caregiver, nutritionist and part-time dentist, you are also his barber! Now you've got a squeaky clean, mat-free, thoroughly dry Mini standing on his grooming table, awaiting his first haircut. If you've trained your Mini to stand politely, you shouldn't have flashbacks of your son's screaming fit at his first trip to the barber shop.

A Miniature Schnauzer in full show coat takes a bit of work, but the end result is worth the effort.

First let's choose the correct size blade for the clipper. You likely will start with the #10 blade, which is suitable for most dogs with a moderately thick coat. If your dog has a thinner coat, the #7F blade works better. Begin by trimming down the back of the neck (from the base of the skull), holding the clipper with the blade against the skin. You can hold the skin taut as you move the clipper smoothly with the grain of the hair. Don't rush or fidget as you can burn the dog and cause skin irritation. Proceed down the back and then trim down the sides of the body to where the chest drops off, about 1.5 inches above the elbow. Be sure to avoid getting too close to the elbow. You want to blend the coat into the under-skirt. Blending the coat requires some practice, but it is not difficult to do; some groomers use the thinning shears to blend between the clippered and scissored areas. Use the clipper in the opposite direction as you go down the sides of the rear legs while folding the furnishings with your other hand. Be careful not to cut off the furnishings. Clipper the front down to the top of the forelegs. Cut hair on the underarms.

By using the clipper backwards (against the grain), you get a closer cut. This is how you want to clipper on the throat and side of the head. Trim the top of the head (between the ears and the eyes, but not the eyebrows!), using the #10 or #15 against the grain of the hair. Now oil the clipper and change the blade to the #30. Always keep the device well oiled so that it doesn't get too hot.

With the #30 blade, proceed to the rear and underside of tail, clippering against the grain. Now for the belly: trim with the same blade (or the #40), leaving about 1.5 inches at the front of the dog, and taper toward the belly button. This is a delicate area for the dog, and be especially careful as you trim around the genital region. Be sure to leave a little fringe over the loin.

The ears are an important feature for the Mini: clipper them with the #40 blade. For the outside of the ear, clipper with the grain and for the inside clipper against the grain. You can tweeze any stray hairs inside the ear as well.

While you're in the middle of the grooming process, don't forget to talk to your dog and give him encouragement. You need to convince him that he's a good boy and that he looks handsome. Give him a little treat now and then to reward him for his patience.

You can use the #40 also to clipper the hair between the pads of the feet. Some groomers prefer to use the scissors for this. Using your comb, go through the hair around the foot and scissor a circle around the foot, trimming hair upwards at a 45-degree angle from the pad. You want the legs to have the desired column-like effect, so fluff the hair around the front legs with the comb to make it stand out. Then carefully scissor and comb in a circular fashion, using the scissors pointing down. In the same manner, proceed to the chest hair, fluffing it out, scissoring it even to where the chest drops off. Trim the hind feet the same as the fore. Trim the rear leg hair carefully so that the hair on the stifle (knee) blends with the hair on the hock (ankle), accenting the leg's contour. Blend the furnishings with the underbelly where the rear leg starts: extend the line of the underbelly into the rear furnishings, not too high up on the side. Comb the hair on the inside of the rear legs and trim to form an inverted "V," with the hair tapering from the inner thigh down to the foot. Trim with the scissors to achieve a straight line

The rectangular appearance of the head, with its width diminishing slightly from the topskull to the nose, is reinforced by correct trimming. You can shape the dog's eyebrows with your scissors and the beard just

enough to complete the rectangular effect. Before trimming the eyebrows, wet them a little bit with water or gel. You want to trim the eyebrow's outer edge in line with the skull's widest part. Then place the scissors behind the corner of the eye, pointing the blade tips toward the nose's center, and cut straight. Next scissor a "V" shape above the dog's nose to create a diamond shape between the eyes. Do not cut out any hair beneath the eyes, as this will result in an unappealing expression. Trim a finger's width at the outside cover of each eye.

Now for the beard: comb it all forward and then take your scissors and trim a line from the widest part of the head. Don't cut too much, and avoid trimming the top portion. For the sides, cut parallel to the skull so that you're not holding the scissors pointing toward the beard itself. Never use the clipper on the bridge of the dog's nose, as it will give the dog an ugly appearance.

Grooming the Mini Schnauzer

PEDICURE

Your dog's nails should be kept short and tidy. The guillotine-type nail clipper is favored by many groomers as it's easy to use. One quick clip and you're moving on to the next nail. Introduce the puppy to his pedicure at an early age. You probably will clip the nails once a month, unless your dog walks daily on rough pavement that naturally wears down his nails. Another handy option is the battery-operated nail grinder with a sandpaper head. The grinder offers the advantage of never cutting into the quick of the nail (the blood vessel in the center of the nail pad). Mini owners should be aware that the dog's hair around his foot can get caught in the grinder if you're not very careful. A styptic pencil or powder should be kept on hand if you're using a nail clipper just in case you cut into the quick.

GROOMING THE MINI SCHNAUZER

Overview

- The wiry coat of the Miniature Schnauzer requires special attention to stay in proper condition.
- Pet grooming is easier than grooming the coat of a show Mini Schnauzer, but both require knowledge of how to do it properly and practice.
- The American Miniature Schnauzer Club's website offers helpful grooming instruction for owners. You can also seek advice from your breeder or a professional groomer with experience in the breed.
- A grooming table, along with brushes, combs, clippers, scissors and nail trimmers, are among the grooming equipment that you will need.
- Bathe the Miniature Schnauzer as needed and trim his nails about once a month.

Home Care for the Mini Schnauzer

Every home with a pet should have a pet first-aid kit. You can acquire all of the items that you'll need and keep them in a kit, along with your vet's and emergency phone numbers, in a place where you can readily access it. Here are the basic items you will need:

• Alcohol for cleaning a wound;

• Antibiotic salve for treating the wound;

• Over-the-counter eye wash in case your dog gets something in his eyes or just needs to have his eyes

An essential part of your dog's home-care routine is his dental care. Poor dental health can cause much more serious diseases, so practice good preventive medicine with your Miniature Schnauzer.

cleaned "to get the red out";

- Forceps for pulling out wood ticks, thorns and burs;
- Styptic powder for when a toenail has been trimmed too short and bleeds;
- A rectal thermometer;
- A nylon stocking to be used as a muzzle if your pet should be badly injured.

Many of these items can be purchased very reasonably from your local drug store. Once your dog is mature and remaining well, he will only need a yearly visit to the veterinary clinic for a check-up and a booster shot for his vaccines. During these visits, the veterinarian will also give your dog a complete dental exam, and you may ask him to express the dog's anal glands, if needed.

You should purchase dental-care items to clean the dog's teeth yourself in between trips to the vet. Set the dog on the grooming table, with his head secured by the leash, and gently scrape

Know basic first-aid techniques so you can deal with minor emergencies such as bee stings, insect bites and other situations that your Mini Schnauzer may encounter outdoors.

Proper chew toys keep your Miniature Schnauzer's mouth happily occupied while providing dental benefits by helping to scrape away tartar as he chews.

away any tartar. Some animals will let you do this and others will not. Regardless, you can use a small toothbrush and canine toothpaste daily or at least weekly. A hard dog treat at bedtime will also help to keep the tartar down.

As for anal glands, expressing them is not the greatest of tasks, besides being quite smelly. You may find that it is easier to have this done during the yearly trip to the clinic. On occasion, the anal glands will become impacted and require veterinary attention to clean out.

By now you know your dog well. You know how much he eats and sleeps and how hard he plays. As with all of us, on occasion he may "go off his feed" or appear to be sick. If he has been nauseated for 24 to 36 hours, has had diarrhea for the same amount of time or has drunk excessive water

for five or six days, a trip to the veterinarian is in order. Make your appointment and tell the receptionist why you need the appointment now.

The veterinarian will ask you the following questions:
- When did he last eat a normal meal?
- How long has he had diarrhea or been vomiting?
- Has he eaten anything in the last 24 hours?
- Could he have eaten a toy or a piece of clothing or anything else unusual?
- Is he drinking more water than usual?

The vet will check him over, take his temperature and pulse, listen to his heart, feel his stomach for any lumps, look at his gums and teeth for color and check his eyes and ears. He will probably also draw blood to run tests.

At the end of the examination, he will make a diagnosis and suggest treatment. He may send your dog home with you with some antibiotics, take some x-rays or keep the dog overnight for observation. Follow your vet's instructions and you will find that very often your dog will be

Parasites can be a problem and there are certain ones of which you should be aware. Heartworm can be a deadly problem, and some parts of the country can be more prone to this than others. Heart-

Consider your Miniature Schnauzer's safety while traveling. A dog should never be allowed to roam freely about a moving vehicle, so his crate is a safe way to keep him confined in the car.

back to normal in a day or two. In the meantime, feed him light meals and keep him quiet, perhaps confined to his crate.

worms become very massive and wrap themselves around the heart. If not treated, the dog will eventually die. In the spring, call your veterinarian and ask if your dog should have a heartworm test. If so, take him to the clinic and he will be given a test to make certain that he is clear of heartworm. Then he will be put on heartworm preventive if recommended by your vet. This is important, particularly if you live in areas where mosquitoes are present.

Fleas are also a problem, particularly in the warmer parts of the country. You can purchase flea powders or a flea collar from the pet-supply shop or ask your veterinarian what he suggests that you use; there are various effective monthly topical treatments to control fleas, ticks and other pests. If you suspect fleas, lay your dog on his side, separate the coat to the skin and look for anything skipping, jumping or skittering around.

Ticks are more prevalent in areas where there are numerous trees. Ticks are small (to start) and dark and like to attach themselves to the warm parts of the ear, the leg pits, the face folds,

A greatly enlarged illustration of the dog flea— a pest with which most pet owners do battle at some time in their pets' lives.

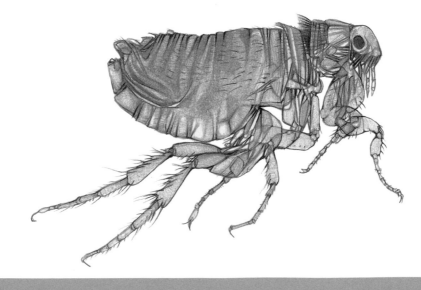

etc. The longer they are on the dog, the bigger they become, filling themselves with your pet's blood and becoming as big as a dime. Take your forceps and carefully pull the tick out to make sure you get the pincers. Promptly flush the tick down the toilet or light a match to it. Put alcohol on the wound and a dab of antibiotic salve.

Let common sense and a good veterinarian be your guide in coping with all of the issues mentioned and all other health problems.

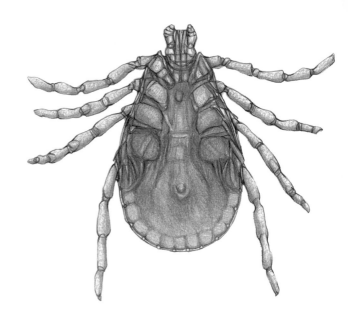

A tick's eight legs give it the strength to burrow in and hold on, which is why ticks are so difficult to remove.

HOME CARE FOR THE MINI SCHNAUZER

Overview

- Have a well-stocked canine first-aid kit so you will be prepared if emergency situations occur.
- "Good housekeeping" for your dog at home includes dental care, checking the condition of the anal glands and parasite control.
- Know your dog well so you can recognize signs of a problem and get veterinary attention right away.
- Protect your dog from parasites, both internal and external, which can compromise his health.

CHAPTER 13

Keeping Your Mini Schnauzer Active

Basic obedience training forms the foundation for success in competitive dog sports.

Many owners and their dogs are looking for something challenging. There are many activities to keep both of you very busy, active and interested. Mini Schnauzers excel in many activities because of their intelligence and ability to learn. After puppy kindergarten, you may want to work toward a Canine Good Citizen® Award. This is a program which, when successfully completed, shows that your dog will mind his manners at home, in public places and with other dogs. This class is available to all dogs (pure or mixed breed) of any age. It's a fun course and useful for everyday life.

There are ten steps, including accepting a friendly stranger, sitting politely for petting, accepting light grooming and examination from a stranger, walking on a loose lead, coming when called, responding calmly to another dog, responding to distractions, down on command and remaining calm when the owner is out of sight for three minutes. Upon successful completion, you will receive an AKC Canine Good Citizen® certificate.

In an advanced obedience exercise, the dog must use scent discrimination to select the right dumbbell from a group and then return it to his handler.

Obedience is a long-established sport in which Mini Schnauzers can excel. Obedience trials are held either by themselves or in conjunction with an AKC conformation show. There are many levels, starting with Novice, where, upon completion of three passing "legs," the dog will earn a Companion Dog (CD) title. The courses

Swimming is wonderful low-stress exercise for all kinds of dogs! This Mini Schnauzer enjoys a dip in the family pool.

then progress in difficulty, with Open at the second level. The dog earns a Companion Dog Excellent (CDX) upon completion of three successful legs. The next class is Utility, which will include off-lead work, silent hand signals and picking the right dumbbells from a group of dumbbells. Not many dogs reach this level. It is a major accomplishment for both owner and dog when a Utility Dog (UD) degree is achieved. The first Miniature Schnauzer to earn a UD was Ch. Mein Herr Schnapps UD, whose owner wrote, "A trained dog is a joy!" Since the 1950s, over 125 Minis have had titles in both conformation and obedience and 15 have had conformation championships and Utility degrees.

Agility testing, started in England, has caught on like wildfire in the US and can be easily found at dog shows. Look for the large, noisy ring filled with competitors and dogs running the course and excited spectators watching at ringside, joining in with cheers.

Dogs are taught to run a course that includes hurdles, ladders, jumps and a variety of challenges. There are a number of degrees in agility, depending upon the obstacles that the dog is able to conquer. AKC defines agility as, "The enjoyment of bringing together communication, training, timing, accuracy and just plain fun in the ultimate game for you and your dog." The sport is lots of exercise and fun for both dog and owner, whether you train recreationally or progress to competitive levels.

Miniature Schnauzers are also eligible for earthdog tests for go-to-ground terriers. There are four class levels: Introduction to Quarry, Junior Earthdog, Senior Earthdog and Master Earthdog. This is a challenging sport for dog and master, testing the abilities and functions for which the Mini Schnauzer was bred.

The ultimate in degrees is

the Versatile Companion Dog. This is the degree that recognizes those dogs and handlers who have been successful in multiple dog sports. In order to excel at any of the aforementioned activities, it is essential to belong to a dog club where there is equipment and facilities for practice. These sports have become so popular with the public that there should be little difficulty in finding a training facility. You will find it a great experience, working with your dog and meeting new people with whom you will have a common interest. This will all take time and interest on your part, and a willing dog working on the other end of the leash.

Mini Schnauzers fare well in competitive canine sports like agility and obedience. Their intelligence, trainability and agility are keys to success.

KEEPING YOUR MINI SCHNAUZER ACTIVE

Overview

- The Miniature Schnauzer is an active and intelligent breed whose body and mind need to be kept busy and challenged.
- The Canine Good Citizen® program awards certificates to dogs who pass a series of exercises that assess general behavior.
- Miniature Schnauzers have reached high degrees of success in competitive obedience and agility.
- A member of the Terrier Group, the Mini Schnauzer is eligible to participate in earthdog events.
- Whatever you choose to do with your Mini Schnauzer, a breed club or training club can help you get started.

Your Mini Schnauzer and His Vet

Your adult Miniature Schnauzer will need to visit his vet anually for his boosters and check-ups.

Before bringing your pup home, the breeder will already have had certain cosmetic procedures done on the puppy. Dewclaws (the fifth nail that comes out on the rear part of the leg above the paw) are removed. Tails are docked. Both procedures are done at the same time on the third or fourth day after birth. If ears are cropped, this is done at around 9 to 11 weeks by a veterinarian who is familiar with cropping Miniature Schnauzer ears. The ears are taped while they are healing, and the vet as well as your breeder will tell you what kind of after-care you need to give for proper healing.

Ear cropping consists of the ear leather's being surgically trimmed and then trained to stand upright. Originally, cropping was done to prevent the ears from being bitten by any adversary. With the fighting dogs and vermin hunters like terriers, it gave the opponent less to hang onto. Ear cropping is also considered by many to be esthetically appealing, as it gives the dog a smart look. However, as it is no longer necessary, many countries have banned ear cropping. In the US, although most Mini Schnauzers are cropped, it is not required.

Before you bring your pup home, you must find a good veterinarian. Your breeder, if from your area, should be able to recommend someone. Otherwise, it will be your

Healthy puppies start with healthy parents, and good breeders do all they can to ensure that their breeding dogs are in top condition and genetically sound.

Very young pups are started off with deworming and their first shots from the breeder, and then the vet takes over when the pups go to their new homes.

job to find a clinic that you like and arrange an appointment for your new pup within his first few days at home.

A major consideration in finding a veterinarian is to find someone convenient, preferably within 10 miles of your home. Find a veterinarian whom you like and trust, and be confident that he knows what he is doing with Mini Schnauzers. See that the office looks and smells clean. It is your right to check on fees before setting up an appointment, and you will usually need an appointment. If you have a satisfactory visit, take the business card so that you have the clinic's number and the name of the veterinarian that you saw. Try and see the same vet at each visit, as he whom personally know the history of your dog and your dog will be familiar with him.

Inquire if the clinic takes emergency calls. If they do not, as many no longer do, get the name, address and telephone number of the emergency veterinary service in your area and keep this with your veterinarian's phone number.

At your pup's first visit to the vet, take along the records from your breeder that document his health, including the shots that your puppy has had, so the veterinarian will know which series of shots your pup should be getting. You should also take in a fecal sample for a worm test.

The recommended vaccines are for distemper, infectious canine hepatitis, leptospirosis, parvovirus infections and parainfluenza. Although this seems like an impressive list of shots, there is one shot that will cover all of these viruses...DHLPP. This series of shots will start between six and ten weeks, which means that the breeder will be giving the first shots to the litter and you will have your vet finish up the series of three shots, given at four-week intervals.

Distemper, at one time, was the scourge of dog breeding, but with the proper immunization and a clean puppy-rearing area, this no longer presents a problem to the reputable breeder. Canine hepatitis, very rare in the United States, is a severe liver infection caused by a virus. Leptospirosis is an uncommon disease that affects the kidneys. It is rare in young puppies, occurring

Make sure that your Miniature Schnauzer fully enjoys his time outdoors by protecting him from any dangers, such as insects, heat, fertilizers, etc.

primarily in adult dogs. Parvovirus is recognized by fever, vomiting and diarrhea. This is a deadly disease for pups and can spread very easily through their feces. The vaccine is highly effective in prevention.

Miniature Schnauzer

The Miniature Schnauzer does have some genetic problems. Reputable breeders and the American Miniature Schnauzer Club are constantly working to rid the breed of these genetic problems.

Schnauzers are prone to several eye problems: later-onset cataracts, congenital cataracts, progressive retinal atrophy (PRA), sudden acquired retinal degeneration (SARD) and congenital cataracts.

A cataract is an opacity that covers the lens. It is usually white and it can be singular or multiple and of any size or shape. As in humans, the degree of impairment to the sight depends upon the size and location of the cataract. Later-onset cataracts are cataracts that appear in adults between the ages of 18 months and 2 years. Congenital cataracts was previously called congenital juvenile cataracts, as they were present in fetuses and could be seen with "slit-lamp" testing of very young puppies. The AMSC has been working on this genetic problem since the 1960s in order to eliminate it from the breed.

PRA (progressive retinal atrophy) is a slow diminishing of the light-sensing organ in the retina, eventually resulting in total blindness of the dog. This is a complicated and serious disease. Miniature Schnauzer breeders have been working diligently to eliminate PRA from the breed. The presence of SARD (sudden acquired retinal degeneration) causes blindness through atrophy of the retina. Research is fairly new on this disease, but is different from PRA inasmuch as blindness will occur in a few weeks from the onset of the problem. With PRA, the progression to total blindness takes around a year.

The American Miniature Schnauzer Club developed an eye pledge in 1973, and each breeder who signs the eye pledge promises to have PRA and to report the eye examination and pedigree of every Miniature Schnauzer affected with eye problems to the AMSC board. For further and up-to-date information on the eye diseases

Proper weight and good coat condition are reflections of good health and care.

slit-lamp examinations for all puppies, to retire from breeding any dam or sire that has produced a puppy with congenital cataracts or in the Miniature Schnauzer, you should contact the American Miniature Schnauzer Club and they will forward your inquiry to the proper committee. Don't forget to ask your breeder if he has tested his animals for eye problems.

Another disorder that can occur in the Miniature Schnauzer is Legge-Calve-Perthes (also called Perthes). This is a bone-related disease and not a hereditary problem. It is thought to be caused by an injury or possibly a nutritional problem. The disease appears between four and ten months of age and is very painful. The dog will limp on one or both rear legs. Eventually the leg muscles become wasted. There are some treatments for Perthes, which should be discussed with your vet.

Pulmonic stenosis is a congenital heart defect that is a narrowing of the connection between the right heart ventricle and the pulmonary artery. Many dogs live with this problem without ever showing any signs of a heart problem. If the defect is severe, your veterinarian may do a balloon valvuloplasty, which is successful in about 70% of the cases.

Eczema and dermatitis are skin problems that occur in many breeds. They can often be tricky problems to solve. Frequent bathing of the dog will remove his natural skin oils and will cause the problem to worsen. Allergies to food or something in the environment can also cause the problem. Consider asking your vet about homeopathic remedies in addition to conventional methods of treatment.

Although this list of health problems may look daunting, the Miniature Schnauzers is considered to be a healthy breed overall. The problems mentioned do exist in the breed and a buyer should be aware of them. Some of these diseases are rare; most of them only show up very infrequently.

Health guarantees are important, and a responsible breeder will give you a contract that will guarantee your pup against certain congenital defects. This guarantee will be limited in time to six months or one year. If there is a problem, the breeder will possibly replace the pup or offer some refund in his price.

Dorothy Williams of the Dorem Kennel wrote that Miniatures have great stamina and, in fact, will show no signs of illness until they are quite sick, and that they are fighters and will not give up. They are also easy whelpers and most careful and devoted mothers. The responsiveness and intelligence of Miniatures Schnauzers make them ideal for obedience work, enhanced by the fact that they love to please their owners. With Miniature Schnauzers we are lucky, as they can often be very healthy to 12 to 14 years of age. It is not unusual for them to live to 16 years if they have good care.

If you purchased your dog as a pet and do not plan to show the dog, you should consider neutering or spaying. The breeder may even require it. A neutered male will be less aggressive and less likely to lift his leg in the house, and have less of a tendency to mount other dogs (or your leg). A spayed female will not come into season every six months, which is not only very hard on your house but will attract neighboring dogs. Neutering and spaying also offer many health benefits, eliminating or reducing the risk of various cancers and other serious problems.

As your dog starts aging, he will start to slow down. He will not play as hard or

Miniature Schnauzer

as long as he used to and he will sleep more. He will find the sunbeam in the morning hours and take a long nap. At this time, you will probably put him on a senior dog food. Continue to watch his weight, as it is more important than ever not to let your senior citizen become obese. You will notice that his muzzle will become gray. You may see opacities in his eyes, signs of cataracts. As he becomes older, he may become arthritic.

Your senior dog will require more attention to his health and comfort, and more frequent trips to the vet. For all the happiness that your Miniature Schnauzer has given you, isn't the extra effort worth it for your old friend?

YOUR MINI SCHNAUZER AND HIS VET

Overview

- You must find a good vet ahead of time and arrange a new-puppy appointment so that your new Mini sees the vet within the first few days of coming home.
- Mini Schnauzer pups usually have tails docked and dewclaws removed when very young, and ear cropping, when done, happens at two to three months old.
- Your vet will give your pup an overall health check-up and continue with his vaccination program.
- Discuss hereditary problems with your breeder and see documentation of relevant testing on the pups and parents.
- Neutering/spaying is recommended for pet dogs, as the procedure offers many health benefits.
- An older dog will require more attention to his care and more frequent visits to the vet.